PLYMOUTH
GIN

ENJOY THE
ORIGINAL TASTE
OF THIS FINE
TRADITION

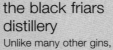

STIL

the secret of plymouth gin's taste

Plymouth Gin's taste and quality are preserved in production standards that stretch back over 200 years.

royal navy links

The Royal Navy has appreciated the taste of Plymouth Gin since the time of Nelson.

SO, WHAT MAKES PLYMOUTH GIN TASTE SO GOOD?

taste of the est country

scover ways to experiment n Plymouth Gin's ceptional flavour in food.

selling plymouth gin

A long tradition of quality in marketing Plymouth Gin has helped preserve its unique character.

the barbican

Plymouth's ancient bustling port is at the heart of Plymouth Gin.

drinking plymouth gin

Discover ways to enjoy the flavour of Plymouth Gin.

Gin is defined as a clear unaged alcohol further distilled with a selection of roots, berries and herbs known as the botanicals. It is one of the world's great drinks, a particularly English drink. Amongst the classic gins such as Beefeater and Tanqueray, Plymouth Gin is unique because the standard designation 'London Dry' is missing from the label. Plymouth Gin is 'Plymouth Dry', the only gin in the world with its own 'appellation controllée', the result of successful court actions brought by producers Coates & Co. to prevent other distillers making 'Plymouth' Gin. By law, Plymouth Gin can only be distilled within the city walls of Plymouth.

The history of Coates & Co.'s Plymouth Gin goes back to 1793, when a young Mr. Coates got involved in the distilling trade at Southside Street in the Barbican, Plymouth's ancient heart. Plymouth Gin's long history is intertwined with Plymouth's rich past, that of an ancient seaport and naval base forever associated with the decisive events that created the nation we live in today.

This book tells the story of Plymouth Gin. Most of all it explains how the taste of our unique gin developed and, just as importantly, how it was preserved through the centuries. For it is the taste of Plymouth that makes it special – the taste of the sea, the taste of exotic ingredients from all over the world, a taste created through a long tradition of quality, care and craftsmanship.

BACKGROUND IMAGE The earliest surviving Plymouth Gin label, registered in the United States in 1881 and in the United Kingdom in 1882.

An Interesting Past

THE PRACTICE OF FLAVOURING ALCOHOL WITH JUNIPER
ALMOST CERTAINLY DATES TO THE ELEVENTH CENTURY WHEN
BENEDICTINE MONKS AT THE RENOWNED MEDICAL SCHOOL
OF SALERNO, ITALY, DISTILLED SPIRITS FROM WINE
AND COMBINED THEM WITH VARIOUS HERBS, ROOTS, FRUITS
AND BERRIES TO MAKE MEDICINES.

1497 John Cabot
discovers Newfoundland.

1509 Henry VIII becomes king.

1517 Martin Luther nails his '95 Theses' to church
door at Wittenberg. Protestant Reformation begins.

1492 Large quantities of grain spirit
being produced in the Low Countries.

Methods of Distillation, illustration from 'Kleines Distillierbuch', 1500 by Hieronymus Brunschwig (1450-c.1512). Distilling is an ancient art that was brought to mainland Europe by Arab scholars as long ago as the 3rd century AD. Indeed al-ko-hol is an Arabic word.

How the taste of Plymouth Gin developed is directly related to the story of gin.

Dr. Sylvius, Professor of Medicine at Leyden University in Holland, recorded a recipe for jenever as a cure for kidney complaints, gout and lumbago but it is unlikely that he was the first to combine grain spirit and juniper. Dutch records from 1492 onwards show significant quantities of grain spirit being produced. It combined well with the juniper growing everywhere in the Low Countries. By the mid 1500s there was already a thriving jenever manufacturing industry.

Juniper elixirs were prized during the years of the Black Death when almost a quarter of Europe's population died from bubonic plague. It was believed that the magical juniper protected against the deadly disease. People not only consumed it but wore masks filled with juniper berries to breathe in its vapours.

In the Low Countries, from the late fifteenth century onwards, juniper flavouring met grain spirit in a new invention, jenever, christened so from the French for juniper – genièvre. Throughout the sixteenth and seventeenth centuries jenever distilleries sprang up in every sizeable town throughout what is now Belgium, Holland and northern France. It became the national drink.

BACKGROUND IMAGE View of the Groothoofdspoort from the north-east, Dordrecht, 1618 by Aelbert Cuyp (1620-91).

Woman drinking with soldiers, 1658
by Pieter de Hooch (1629-84).

1529 Henry VIII fails to get consent from the Pope to divorce Catherine of Aragon.

1533 Henry VIII marries Anne Boleyn and is excommunicated by the Pope.

1543 Henry VIII marries Anne Parr, his sixth wife.

1547 Edward VI becomes king.

1539 Dissolution of the Monastries including Plymouth's White Friars and Grey Friars establishments.

King William III by William Wissing (1656-87).

Gathering the Golden Grain, near Bishopsteighton, Plymouth by John Barrett.

When William arrived in England he landed at Brixham, near Plymouth. Plymouth was the first English town to recognise him as King. William was a stern, serious man except, as his Dutch page recorded, when 'he was sharing a bottle of jinever with his compatriots'. It is believed that some of his retainers remained in Plymouth and set up a jenever distillery.

William III died in 1702, from injuries received from a fall from his horse which stumbled over a mole hill.

BACKGROUND IMAGE *William III and Mary II.*

In England jenever was well known to soldiers and sailors who had fought in the long European wars of the seventeenth century. They encountered Dutch Courage given as morale boosting drams before battle and brought the taste for it home. The great sea ports of London, Liverpool, Bristol and, of course, Plymouth, soon became centres for drinking jenever brought in from the Low Countries.

But jenever, geneva, or gin as it was known by now, was still not commonly drunk. Indeed spirits were not commonly drunk in England at this time. What changed all this was the arrival of Dutch William of Orange on the British throne in 1688. His Glorious Revolution was also a revolution in drinking culture as legislation was immediately introduced to restrict imports of French wine and brandy and encourage the development of domestic distilling using 'good English corn'. There was already a clear demand for gin in the most populous cities and, because it was the preferred drink of William and his court, drinking gin soon became both fashionable and patriotic. And so an industry was born.

1553 Mary I becomes queen.   1558 Elizabeth I becomes queen.   1567 Mary Queen of Scots forced to abdicate and imprisoned a year later by Elizabeth I.

c.1565 Dr. Sylvius of Leyden records recipe for 'eau de vie de genievre' later jenever.   c.1572 First commercial jenever distillery founded by Lucas Bols.

Snuff and Gin by Thomas Rowlandson.

The Spa Fields Orator Hunt-ing for Popularity to Do-Good! by George Cruikshank, 1817. One of his demands was the reform of the gin industry.

In 1730, in some parts of London, one house in three sold gin.

FACING PAGE *Gin Lane*, 1751 by William Hogarth.

BACKGROUND IMAGE *Every Man has his Hobby Horse*, 1784. Satire on British desire for gin in Georgian times.

During the first decades of the eighteenth century English distilling became a free for all. Legal and illegal production rocketed leading to the years of gin mania, particularly in London, where the hospitals, courts and workhouses were said to be filled with people ruined by their addiction to gin. Finally, after several spectacularly unsuccessful attempts to reform the fledgling industry, the first piece of sensible legislation was introduced in 1751. In 1756 further legislation controlled who could make gin and who could sell it. It also introduced excise duties on gin which then increased steadily. By the 1790s the days of cheap gin were over. Proper regulation of the distilling trade drove the unscrupulous out and attracted reputable businessmen. Now begins the rise of the great gin brands that are still household names today – Coates & Co.'s Plymouth Gin amongst them.

1577 Alliance between England and Netherlands.

1587 Mary Queen of Scots executed.
1588 Spanish Armada defeated.

1577 Drake completes his voyage of circumnavigation.

1581 Drake becomes Mayor of Plymouth.

1590 Work begins on the Plymouth Leat, sponsored by Drake, Britain's first municipal water supply.

The Gin Shop, a plate from *The Drunkard's Children*, 1848 by George Cruikshank.

Samuel Johnson, the famous 18th century social commentator wryly remarked on the rise of distilling 'the trade of distilling is the most profitable in the Kingdom except that of being broker to the prime minister'.

A new, clear style of gin developed. The invention of the continuous still meant that pure spirit could be produced efficiently. There was now no need to mask the flavours of rough alcohol with sugar and strong spices. Instead the spirit could be gently enhanced with delicate flavourings. This style came to be known as London Dry because most distillers were based in London. At the same time, the ports of Liverpool, Bristol and Plymouth created their own versions of a more aromatic and fruity 'dry' gin. Of them all, Plymouth Gin alone survives, its unique character preserved in the long tradition of craftsmanship at the Black Friars Distillery, its unique status enshrined in English law.

In 1730 official gin production in London had reached 11 million gallons – 14 gallons for every member of the population. In 1736 Parliament passed the first Gin Act to try and control gin production It was extremely unpopular and led to riots all over the country. Mock funeral processions mourning the death of 'Madam Geneva' took place in the streets of London, Bristol and Plymouth, the great gin drinking hubs. The Act was completely ineffective and gin consumption continued to soar.

BACKGROUND IMAGE *The Gin Juggarnarth* by George Cruikshank. A satire on gin's apparent grip on British life in the early nineteenth century.

The GIN JUGGARNATH or The Worship of the GREAT SPIRIT of the age

GIN PRODUCING CITIES, 1750

1. Plymouth	3. London	5. Warrington
2. Bristol	4. Norwich	6. Liverpool

Plymouth
a Special Place

THE STARTING POINT FOR COUNTLESS JOURNEYS OF ADVENTURE
AND THE GREAT DISCOVERY THAT IS THE TASTE OF PLYMOUTH GIN.

A *View of the Tamar Estuary, Plymouth* by Thomas L. Hornbrook.

Plymouth's first inhabitants were groups of fisher-folk gathered around the mouth of the River Plym in Sutton. As the fishing industry expanded so did local ship-building expertise and facilities, enabling the local fishermen to take their ships further and further abroad. At this time Sutton was also known as Plymouth and was already an important port.

Sir Francis Drake by Samuel Lane.

Drake was playing his famous game of bowls on Plymouth Hoe when news of the arrival of the Spanish Armada reached him. His remark that there was time to finish the game and beat the Spaniards too was probably motivated by the knowledge that the tide would not allow his ships to sail for some hours in any case.

The Armada by Nicholas Hilliard, 1588.

The Armada left Lisbon on 28th May 1588, with 130 ships and 19,000 men.

BACKGROUND IMAGE An English ship from 1609.

The city of Plymouth began its association with the Royal Navy in 1294 when Edward I assembled the first ever English fleet here during one of the many territorial wars between England and France. Throughout the Middle Ages Plymouth prospered, its wealth based on continental trade.

Later, Elizabethan Plymouth was an exciting, if somewhat lawless place. From its harbour the buccaneers John Hawkins and Francis Drake embarked on long voyages returning to Plymouth laden with treasure from the New World, looted from the Spanish and Portuguese. When war with Spain came, Drake was Vice Admiral of the British fleet as it sailed from Plymouth Sound to defeat the Spanish Armada in 1588, a momentous date in English history.

During the Napoleonic Wars Plymouth was one of the ports of Admiral Nelson's naval force as it set out to fight in the famous victories of the Nile and Trafalgar. Plymouth has been the starting point for other journeys of adventure including Captain Cook's voyages to the Antipodes and Darwin's expedition to the Galapagos Islands. The first European ships to reach Australia, New Zealand and Nova Scotia left from Plymouth as did Captain Scott's voyage to the South Pole.

1625 Charles I becomes king. 1629 Charles I dissolves Parliament.

1642 The Battle of Edgehill marks
the beginning of the Civil War.   1649 Charles I executed.

1638 Charles I grants the monopoly of English distilling
to the London based Company of Distillers.

1643 Royalist forces defeated at
the Battle of Freedom Fields, Plymouth.

A director of Coates & Co. photographed for a
Picture Post article about Plymouth recovering
from World War II.

The first woman Member of Parliament, Nancy Astor, became MP for Plymouth Central
in the by-election of 1919.

There were 59
German air raids
on Plymouth,
destroying 3,754
houses and
damaging 8,000.

Plymouth has had its dark days too. The darkest were during the
Second World War when, because of its important dockyard, the city
was subjected to relentless German bombing. Plymouth town centre
and docks were virtually destroyed in the Blitz of March and June 1941.

Throughout the Second World War look-outs were posted on the roof
of the distillery to watch for German bombs. When Southside Street was
hit, great care was taken to ensure that the distillery itself was saved and
could continue to operate. It remained open for business throughout
the war but rationing made it hard to obtain ingredients to make
Plymouth Gin and its export market suffered. However, both Plymouth
Gin and the city have always had the ability to overcome adversity.

BACKGROUND IMAGE The Plymouth Gin label for
the home trade, used between 1910 and 1953.

FACING PAGE Plymouth after Luftwaffe bombing
during the Second World War.

1651 Charles II defeated at Battle of Worcester.
1653 Oliver Cromwell becomes Lord Protector.
1660 Charles II restored to the throne.
1665 Great Plague of London.
1666 Great Fire of London.

1663 Samuel Pepys is prescribed juniper flavoured spirit.
1666 The foundation stone of Plymouth Citadel is laid.

A Snug Cabin or *Port Admiral* by Thomas Rowlandson, c.18th century. Note the stone jars of gin in the two baskets.

Euryalus, Thunderer and *Ajax* leaving Plymouth on the way to Cadiz and the Battle of Trafalgar, 1805, by Thomas Buttersworth.

Plymouth Gin and The Royal Navy

The city of Plymouth has always been crucial to Britain's ability to rule the waves. William III, who did so much for British drinking habits, founded the Naval Dockyard at Devonport in 1691 and ever since the city has been the home of the Royal Navy. Not surprisingly Plymouth Gin has been the Navy's favourite tipple for centuries. Around the time of the Napoleonic Wars, whilst ordinary seamen received regular rations of beer or rum on long voyages, naval officers developed a taste for gin, particularly Plymouth Gin, a reminder of home.

The gin drinking of the Navy considerably enhanced gin's prestige as it climbed the ladder of respectability in Victorian times. By 1850 Coates & Co. were supplying over 1000 barrels of 'navy strength' 57% abv gin a year to the Royal Navy who put it to very good use. Two classic gin drinks were invented by enterprising naval surgeons. The Pink Gin, or 'Pinkers'

BACKGROUND IMAGE **Lord Horatio Nelson.**

1679 Act of Habeas Corpus passed, forbidding imprisonment without trial.　**1685** James VIII of Scotland becomes James II of England.　**1688** 'Glorious Revolution' William III of Orange invited to take English throne.　**1694** Foundation of the Bank of England.

1690 First Act of Parliament to encourage distilling from corn - monopoly abolished, distilling open to all.　　**1694** Duty on beer increased and spirits become cheaper than beer.

Winston Churchill welcoming home HMS *Exeter*, Plymouth 1943.
Plymouth Gin was particularly important to the Royal Navy during the Second World War. After the German blitz on Plymouth an Admiralty message was sent to all ships telling of the destruction of the city but rejoicing that the Black Friars Distillery had survived.

A Commissioning Kit.
In the 1960s R. T. Harris, MD of Coates & Co. presented a number of luxurious privately owned American yachts with Commissioning Kits. He was unable to present the kits to US Navy ships as they were 'dry' at sea.

During the Falkland conflict the wartime tradition was revived when Plymouth Gin was presented to any Royal Navy ship sinking an enemy ship. Here, HMS *Alacrity* is one of five British vessels who received cases of Plymouth Gin from head distiller Desmond Payne.

The Royal Navy has appreciated the taste of Plymouth Gin since the time of Nelson.

BACKGROUND IMAGE Embarkation of the Prince of Wales in HMS *Hero* at Plymouth for Canada.

as it fondly became known, was first made by adding a few drops of angostura bitters, normally used as a preventative against tropical disease, to a jigger of neat Plymouth Gin. The second, the Gimlet, came about when a clever ship's doctor named Gimlette realised just how much better the daily ration of lime juice (given to prevent scurvy) tasted with the addition of a measure or two of Plymouth Gin.

Royal Navy ships spread the fashion for drinking gin around the world. Because of the close links between the Navy and Plymouth Gin, the green and white flag hoisted as an invitation to 'come aboard for a drink' became known throughout the Fleet as the Gin Pennant. Wherever the Navy went, demand for Plymouth Gin soared.

Today Plymouth Gin's connections with the Royal Navy are as strong as ever. Every new ship of the line still receives a Plymouth Gin Commissioning Kit – a handsome wooden box containing the Gin Pennant, glasses, a gurgling fish jug and, of course, a bottle or two of Navy Strength Plymouth Gin.

1702 William III dies,
Queen Anne succeeds.

1707 Act of Union between Scotland & England,
seat of Scottish Government transfers to London.

1714 Queen Anne dies and
George I succeeds to the throne.

1721 Sir Robert Walpole becomes Britain's
first Prime Minister, stays in power until 1742.

1700 Duty paid on spirits doubled in 10 years.

1709 Rudyerd's lighthouse built on Eddystone Reef to replace
Winstanley's lighthouse, which was swept away in a storm in 1703.

1720 The Mutiny Act excused distillers
from having soldiers billeted on them.

Sir John Hawkins.

The Pilgrim Fathers leave for America
aboard the *Mayflower*, 1620.

Mayflower Steps.

The Barbican

The Barbican was the water-gate of the medieval castle that once
protected the entrance to Sutton Harbour. In Tudor times the term
came to apply to the whole port area. Then it was the place to be.
Sir Francis Drake lived there and nearby lived his friend and fellow
buccaneer, Sir John Hawkins. Sir Walter Raleigh was a frequent visitor.

After the Civil War and subsequent restoration of the monarchy Charles
II extended the old fortifications built by Drake on the Hoe into the
magnificent and impregnable Citadel. A sentinel over the Barbican, it
has been in continuous military occupation since and is currently
home to 29 Commando, Royal Marines.

Below the Citadel once lay cobbled streets overhung with half timbered
Elizabethan houses, crowded quays and the forest of masts belonging to
the hundreds of ships moored in Sutton Harbour.

Plymouth's
ancient bustling
port is at the
heart of
Plymouth Gin.

1726 Jonathan Swift publishes 'Gulliver's Travels'.
1727 George III becomes King.

1739 Britain goes to war with
Spain in the 'War of Jenkin's Ear'.

1745 Jacobite Rebellion in Scotland
led by 'Bonnie Prince Charlie'.

1746 Jacobites crushed at
the Battle of Culloden.

1733 London producing 14 gallons
of gin per year for every resident.

1743 First effective legislation to control
production and sale of gin.

The Custom's House on The Parade, c.1900.

The Barbican, c.1900.

The Barbican,
like all port areas,
was a place for
drinking. In the
19th century
dockers regularly
drank six pints
of beer before
breakfast.

Here was the ancient heart of a mighty seaport with its Guildhall, its Customs House, its fish market, its myriad of chandlers, taverns, eating houses, sailors' lodgings and every conceivable kind of industry from rope making to cooperage. From here in 1620 the Pilgrim Fathers sailed in the Mayflower to start a new life in faraway America where they founded a new Plymouth.

Most importantly for the story of the adventure of Plymouth Gin, the Barbican has always been a centre for trade where, beginning in 1211, exotic cargoes have been landed from all over the world. Later came rare herbs and spices from the East, sugar from the West Indies, oranges and lemons from southern Europe. All the necessary ingredients for gin, arriving on busy wharves, a short step away from Black Friars Distillery in Southside Street.

BACKGROUND IMAGE **The Barbican Fish Market.**

The white circle shows the location of the Black Friars Distillery on a 1820s engraving of Plymouth.

The Black Friars Distillery

LEGEND HAS IT THAT THE DISTILLERY BUILDING IN
SOUTHSIDE STREET WAS THE FORMER MONASTERY OF AN ORDER
OF DOMINICANS, HENCE THE NAME BLACK FRIARS.

1752 Adoption of the Gregorian Calendar in Britain.

1759 Wolfe captures Quebec and expels the French from Canada.　　1769 James Watt patents the Steam Engine.　　1774 Boston Tea Party.

1759 Smeaton's lighthouse replaces Rudyerd's lighthouse, which burnt down on Eddystone Rocks.

1768 Captain Cook sets out from Plymouth aboard the Endeavour.

Inner doorway of Black Friars.
This door leading to the distillery with its ornate stone carving is a beautiful example of the English Perpendicular architectural style.

The Refectory Room at Black Friars is a National Monument. In 1961 it was completely restored and its magnificent high timbered roof returned to its original glory.

Unlike many other gins, Plymouth Gin is still distilled at its original distillery.

THIS EARLY 15TH CENTURY BUILDING FORMED PART OF THE MONASTERY OF THE DOMINICANS OR "BLACK FRIARS"

BACKGROUND IMAGE The plaque outside the distillery explaining the monastery link.

The most intact part of the Black Friars Distillery is the monks' Refectory Room. It is one of the oldest buildings in Plymouth dating from the early 1400s.

Black Friars became in turn the town's Marshalsea or debtor's prison, the first Non-Conformist meeting place and a billet for Huguenot refugees. The Pilgrim Fathers are reputed to have spent their last night in England here before they set sail on the Mayflower.

Black Friars is also indisputably the oldest working gin distillery in the country. A deed of sale dated 12th November 1697 refers to a 'mault-house' on the premises and so it is clear that Black Friars was used for making alcohol from the birth of legal commercial distilling in England. When distilling was deregulated in 1690, malting grain, brewing, distilling and rectifying (the process of re-distilling spirit to make gin) were complementary activities, often carried out under the same roof. Only in 1825 did it become illegal to produce the base spirit and redistilled gin at the same location. Descriptions of Black Friars after that date refer only to a distillery so, obviously, Messrs. Coates' business was now successful enough to focus exclusively on making gin and other 'rectified' spirits.

1775 Start of the American War of Independence.

1783 Britain recognises American independence at the Peace of Versaille.

1789 Outbreak of French Revolution.

1796 Vaccination against smallpox is introduced.

1776 Captain Cook set out from Plymouth on the ill-fated *Resolution*.

1793 First reference to Coates & Co.'s Plymouth Gin.

The copper still that was installed in 1855.

Coopers preparing barrels and boxes to be filled.

Barrels being filled for customers who had their own bottling facilities.

In the late 18th century the area now occupied by the distillery was home to numerous small businesses, many of them drink related. In Broad Hoe Lane were Brittan the brewer, Thomas Putt, a corn factor who would have supplied grain for spirit making and Scott the maltster. In Southside Street there were three distillers including Mr. Coates. Further down the street were Collier, a wine and spirit merchant and two taverns – The Plymouth Arms and The Royal Oak.

Throughout the 19th century Coates & Co. gradually expanded the distillery. A major investment in 1855 saw the installation of a new copper pot-still – the one still used today. In the 1890s land belonging to the former Hoe House was purchased and a splendid new warehouse and manager's house were built. Later an automated bottling line was set up in the warehouse.

During the Second World War German bombs caused a huge fire that destroyed Coates & Co.'s offices in Southside Street and, sadly, much of the old company records and history.

A major investment in 1855 saw the installation of a new copper pot-still – the one still used today.

BACKGROUND IMAGE Sketch of the Black Friars Monastery, published in 1884.

PLYMOUTH GIN

Plymouth Distillery in 1985.

BLACK FRIARS PEOPLE

Distilling is an ancient skill directly handed down from the stillrooms of the great monastic houses throughout medieval Europe. Although distillers today draw on a number of modern techniques to enable efficient production of consistent brand qualities, distilling itself remains an occupation where art and science meet. At Black Friars there have been remarkably few head distillers despite the long history of Coates & Co. In the twentieth century each individual played a key role in ensuring that the distinctive taste of Plymouth Gin was preserved through good times, and bad.

Visitors are astonished by the small number of people who are involved in producing Plymouth Gin today. The 1960s was Black Friars' production heyday when over 50 people were employed making Seager's Gin and Vodka as well as Plymouth Gin. Today 18 people work for the company including tour guides and visitor centre staff.

A dedicated staff safeguarding Plymouth Gin's special taste.

BERT ROBERTS (left)
Plymouth Gin's longest serving employee, Bert joined the distillery in 1935 as the delivery boy when the Freeman family still owned the brand. He retired 47 years later as Distillery Manager and as Plymouth's 'Mr. Gin'. Still living locally, he visits regularly.

SMOND PAYNE (above)
expertise was the steadying hand
e helm of the good ship
nouth Gin throughout the dark
of the 1980s and 90s when the
d was shuffled around the
ks giants' portfolios.

R.T. HARRIS (above)
In charge of Plymouth Gin when it was acquired by Seager Evans in 1958. He reintroduced Commissioning Kits for the Royal Navy and oversaw the return of Plymouth to a 100% grain spirit.

SEAN HARRISON (above)
Plymouth Gin's Head Distiller since 1996. Sean is playing a crucial role in Plymouth Gin's renaissance.

CK BLACKNELL (right)
ed in 2001 and is the current
aging Director of Coates & Co.
role is focused on restoring
nouth Gin to the position it
held when it was known the
d over as England's finest gin.

PAUL CHILARECKI (above)
Joined Plymouth Gin in 1997, after a career in the Royal Navy. He worked first as distillery engineer and is now Plymouth Gin's Production Manager.

PHILIP MILNER (above)
Joined Seager Evans at the age of 15 as an office boy and was Head Distiller at Plymouth in the 1960s when Seager's Gin and Vodka were also made at Black Friars.

CHARLES ROLLS (left)
An established entrepreneur, Charles Rolls became Managing Director of Coates & Co. in March 1997. He was instrumental in the revival of Plymouth Gin, turning it from 5,000 to 50,000 cases in six years.

Coates & Co. allowed only Plymouth Gin that had been made and bottled at Plymouth to be exported. Clear glass bottles to demonstrate the purity of the spirit were specified then and are still used today.

Plymouth Gin was at one time known in China as 'Jossman' because the Plymouth monk bore a striking resemblance to the Chinese figure of good luck.

Tastings in fashionable bars and clubs help to introduce Plymouth Gin to a younger market.

SELLING PLYMOUTH GIN

There has long been a tradition of quality attached to the marketing of Plymouth Gin and great care has always been taken to preserve its unique image and heritage. Although, in the company's very earliest days, gin would have been sold in barrels to spirits merchants who would have bottled it themselves, Coates & Co. were one of the first gin distillers to develop a distinctive look and style for their products. The words 'Plymouth Dry Gin', 'Made in Plymouth' and 'Established in 1793' appear on every bottle of Plymouth Gin and have done for well over a hundred and fifty years. A cheerful monk dressed in black, a reminder of the distillery's monastic past, has been a feature of Plymouth Gin's packaging since around 1870. Today his place has been taken by another Plymouth icon – the Mayflower. The monk is still there however, now strategically positioned in such a way that, when his feet are dry, it's time to buy another bottle.

A long tradition of quality in marketing Plymouth Gin has helped preserve its unique character.

Welcome to Plymouth
Twinned with Tonic

BACKGROUND IMAGE A sign that was put up to promote Plymouth Gin to the 2 million visitors travelling through Plymouth for the 1999 eclipse.

FACING PAGE An advert from the 1970s.

No matter where the Navy sailed, they were never far from Plymouth.

Coates & Co (Plymouth) Ltd., 20 Queen Anne's Gate, London, SW1H 9AA and Blackfriars Distillery, Plymouth.

COATES & CO.
THE BUSINESS

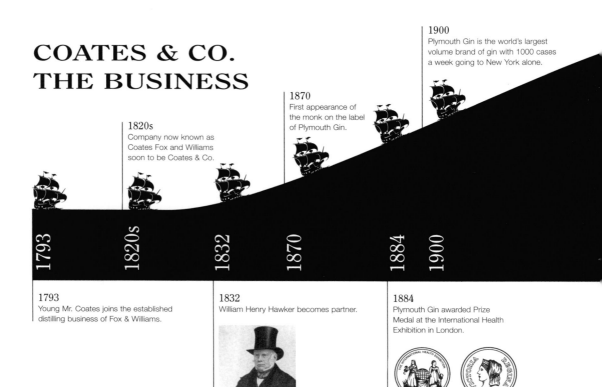

1820s
Company now known as
Coates Fox and Williams
soon to be Coates & Co.

1870
First appearance of
the monk on the label
of Plymouth Gin.

1900
Plymouth Gin is the world's largest
volume brand of gin with 1000 cases
a week going to New York alone.

1793   1820s   1832   1870   1884   1900

1793
Young Mr. Coates joins the established
distilling business of Fox & Williams.

1832
William Henry Hawker becomes partner.

William Henry Hawker

1884
Plymouth Gin awarded Prize
Medal at the International Health
Exhibition in London.

The business of Coates & Co. dates from 1793, the year it is believed
that a young man by the name of Coates joined two distillers, Fox and
Williams, at Black Friars. A Plymouth Business Directory of 1822
confirms that Coates, Fox and Williams were all operating as distillers
there at this time. Very soon afterwards the enterprising Mr. Coates
is believed to have become the senior partner of the company, now
known as Messrs. Coates & Co.

The 1882 Plymouth Gin label.

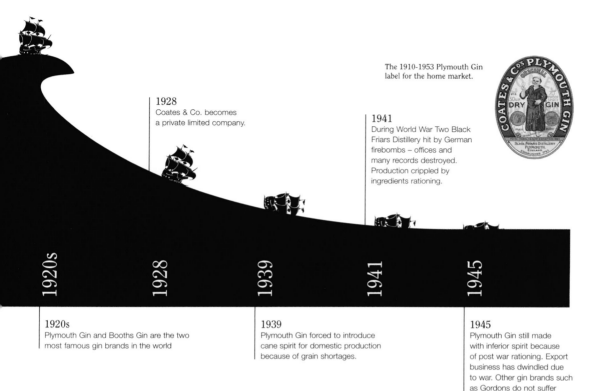

The 1910-1953 Plymouth Gin label for the home market.

1928
Coates & Co. becomes a private limited company.

1941
During World War Two Black Friars Distillery hit by German firebombs – offices and many records destroyed. Production crippled by ingredients rationing.

1920s

1928

1939

1941

1945

1920s
Plymouth Gin and Booths Gin are the two most famous gin brands in the world

1939
Plymouth Gin forced to introduce cane spirit for domestic production because of grain shortages.

1945
Plymouth Gin still made with inferior spirit because of post war rationing. Export business has dwindled due to war. Other gin brands such as Gordons do not suffer because they are already in production around the world.

The six partners, 1909, from left to right, H. Collinssplatt, F. Freeman, F. Lemaur, H.G. Hawker, H. Freeman, H.May.

In 1832 William Henry Hawker Senior joined the business as a partner. His grandson, Francis Ford Freeman, later joined the family firm and for over a hundred and fifty years Coates & Co. was a private company, owned and managed by the closely connected descendants of the Hawker and Freeman families joined by other cousins, the Mays. And it prospered. By 1900 Plymouth Gin had the biggest export market of any UK produced gin and was sold in over 50 countries throughout the world. In 1928 the business became a Limited Company, still with members of the Freeman and Hawker family on the Board.

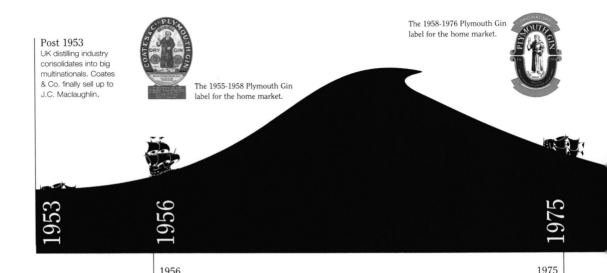

Post 1953
UK distilling industry consolidates into big multinationals. Coates & Co. finally sell up to J.C. Maclaughlin.

The 1955-1958 Plymouth Gin label for the home market.

The 1958-1976 Plymouth Gin label for the home market.

1953

1956

1975

1956
J.C. Maclaughlin sells to American owned Seager Evans.

1975
Whitbread acquired Plymouth Gin when it acquired other Seager brands such as Long John International, the whisky brand. Exclusive distribution rights were retained by Seagers who then ceased to develop Plymouth Gin's US market.

The 1959-1964 export label for Plymouth Gin.

Plymouth Gin delivery vehicles for London.

After the war came the first of the large scale reorganisations of the UK distilling industry. Coates & Co. was a minnow in this new world of large conglomerates with their massively increased purchasing and distribution power. In 1953 the family sold out to J.C. Maclaughlin, a noted entrepreneur. In 1956 he sold the company to American owned Seager Evans who made a large scale investment in plant and facilities at Black Friars, now also used for the making of Seager's own brand gin and vodka.

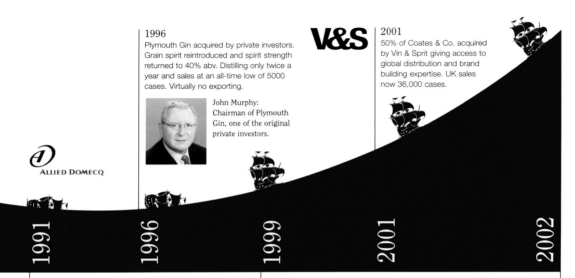

1996
Plymouth Gin acquired by private investors. Grain spirit reintroduced and spirit strength returned to 40% abv. Distilling only twice a year and sales at an all-time low of 5000 cases. Virtually no exporting.

John Murphy: Chairman of Plymouth Gin, one of the original private investors.

V&S

2001
50% of Coates & Co. acquired by Vin & Sprit giving access to global distribution and brand building expertise. UK sales now 36,000 cases.

ALLIED DOMECQ

1991   1996   1999   2001   2002

1991
Whitbread sold Plymouth Gin to Allied Domecq as part of a package that included Beefeater Gin. Plymouth Gin positioned as the inferior cheaper brand, spirit returned to cane spirit and alcoholic strength dropped.

Plymouth Gin label from 1976-1997.

1999
UK sales triple to 18,000 cases and exports rise eight fold. Strength now at the traditional strength of 41.2% abv.

Plymouth Gin labels from 1998-2002.

2002
Vin & Sprit increase their shareholding and Plymouth Gin continues to expand in the world's major gin markets and at home. Domestic sales reach 60,000 cases and export sales are now 30% of production. Plymouth Gin declared No.1 Premium Gin in the UK, outselling Bombay Sapphire and Beefeater, by Impact Magazine.

The current Plymouth Gin labels.

In 1975 Coates & Co. was acquired by Whitbread and Plymouth Gin became part of a complicated 'pass the corporate parcel' game in the hands of brand owners who did not appreciate its traditional values, quality and image. In 1996 Coates & Co. was acquired by a small group of private investors. They had the energy and vision to embark on the regeneration of Plymouth Gin and ensure that it assumed its rightful place as one of the world's oldest, most popular and most respected gins.

Quiet. Refined. Smooth.
Oh, yes, so is the fellow we sent to introduce our gin.

Who better, we thought, to introduce our gin to this country than our man, Simon. After all, he shares the very characteristics you will find in Plymouth Gin. What makes it so refined? Perhaps our stringent botanical selection. Or maybe our long-standing commitment to use only pure Dartmoor water, fresh from the gentle, sloping hills of England. The fact is, there are a number of explanations for Plymouth's supremely smooth taste. Hence, there are an equal number of reasons for you to find Simon and ask him for a sampling. Do so, and you'll discover why Simon thinks his Plymouth Gin is the smoothest tasting gin in the world.

PLYMOUTH GIN. *The gin of taste.*

Plymouth Gin is one of the world's classic gins.

The journey of Plymouth Gin is an adventure with a happy ending. It is now the fastest growing premium gin in the home market. Moreover Plymouth Gin is well on its way to to replicating this success around the world.

Plymouth Gin has expanded into all the key international gin markets – the United States, Canada, Australasia, the Far East, northern and southern Europe and world-wide Duty Free outlets. Once again it is the choice of the sophisticated, discerning drinker who values taste and quality above all else. With new extensions to the range and a choice of alcoholic strengths Plymouth Gin has an exciting future.

The Plymouth Gin range comprises: **Plymouth Gin Original Strength** 41.2% abv, **Plymouth Gin Navy Strength** 57% abv, **Plymouth Damson Liqueur, Plymouth Sloe Gin,** and **Plymouth Classic Fruit Cup.**

PLYMOUTH GIN
NAVY STRENGTH 57% ABV

PLYMOUTH
DAMSON LIQUEUR

PLYMOUTH
SLOE GIN

PLYMOUTH CLASSIC
FRUIT CUP

PLYMOUTH GIN
ORIGINAL STRENGTH 41.2% ABV

FACING PAGE In 2003 the first ever Plymouth Gin advertising campaign was launched in the US specifically targeted at the US consumer base.

The head distiller checking 'the middle cut'.　　The spirit safe.　　The copper still, showing the swan neck.

THE SECRET OF PLYMOUTH GIN'S TASTE

It is appropriate that the Plymouth Gin Distillery should be housed in an ancient and venerable building since Coates & Co.'s production methods have changed little for over two hundred years. Plymouth Gin is a hand-crafted gin unlike many other gins which are mass produced in vast, modern factories.

Into the 155 year old copper still is placed a 96% pure grain spirit, water and the seven botanicals that make up the Plymouth Gin recipe. At Black Friars the water is crystal clear Dartmoor water which runs through peat over granite. Experts claim that this water is the most important element of the exceptionally smooth, fresh taste of Plymouth Gin. A natural resource that no other gin has.

Heat is gently applied until boiling temperature is reached. At this point the spirit, in vapour form, rises slowly up through the high swan neck of the still. As it cools in the attached condenser it becomes liquid again, now imbued with the subtle flavours of the botanical mix.

Plymouth Gin's taste and quality are preserved in production standards that stretch back over 200 years.

BACKGROUND IMAGE An 1898 advert for Plymouth Gin that appeared in the first brochure for Thresher & Co.

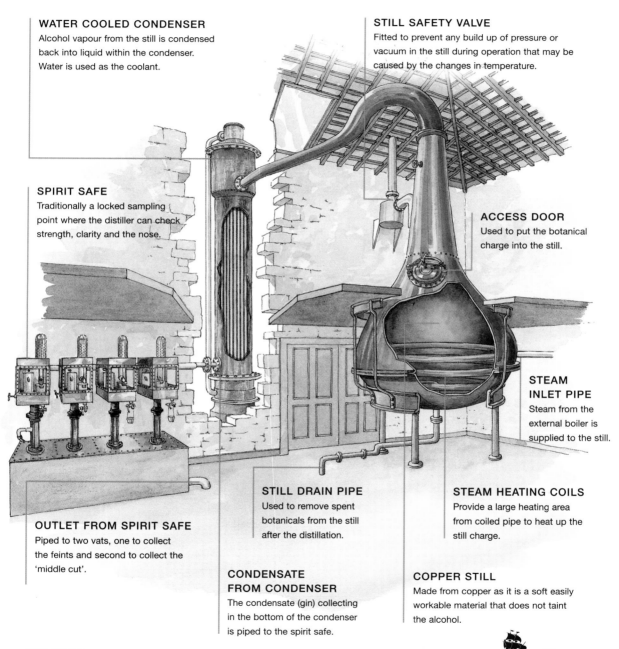

WATER COOLED CONDENSER
Alcohol vapour from the still is condensed back into liquid within the condenser. Water is used as the coolant.

STILL SAFETY VALVE
Fitted to prevent any build up of pressure or vacuum in the still during operation that may be caused by the changes in temperature.

SPIRIT SAFE
Traditionally a locked sampling point where the distiller can check strength, clarity and the nose.

ACCESS DOOR
Used to put the botanical charge into the still.

STEAM INLET PIPE
Steam from the external boiler is supplied to the still.

OUTLET FROM SPIRIT SAFE
Piped to two vats, one to collect the feints and second to collect the 'middle cut'.

STILL DRAIN PIPE
Used to remove spent botanicals from the still after the distillation.

STEAM HEATING COILS
Provide a large heating area from coiled pipe to heat up the still charge.

CONDENSATE FROM CONDENSER
The condensate (gin) collecting in the bottom of the condenser is piped to the spirit safe.

COPPER STILL
Made from copper as it is a soft easily workable material that does not taint the alcohol.

Dartmoor, the source of the water used in Plymouth Gin.

The crystal clear Dartmoor water.

When the spirit reaches the spirit safe the process of constant testing by Plymouth Gin's distilling staff begins. They disregard the first and last parts of the run because they will contain undesirable, strong, oily flavours. The head distiller makes 'the middle cut', as it is called, once he is satisfied that the consistent taste and alcoholic strength he is looking for has been achieved. The exact moment is a trade secret, part of the recipe of Plymouth Gin. Once the cut is made, the gin, as it is now, is diverted via a pipe to the spirit collector and thence to storage vats.

The final stage of making Plymouth Gin is to reduce its alcoholic strength to 41.2% abv by adding water. The water must be exceptionally pure. Since water is a large percentage of the final product, this is a very important part of the production process.

At Black Friars the water is crystal clear Dartmoor water which runs through peat over granite.

PLYMOUTH
GIN

IDEAL FOR COCKTAILS

BACKGROUND IMAGE
An advert for Plymouth Gin from 1935.

THE QUALITY
DRY GIN

Cardamom being selected in Sri Lanka.

Harvesting lemons in southern Spain.

THE BEST BOTANICALS

Its aromatic flavour comes from exotic ingredients imported from far flung corners of the world.

The recipe for Plymouth Gin dates back to the time where traditionally gin made outside London was less juniper dominated, more aromatic and more rounded in flavour. It specifies seven botanicals commonly used in gin production but their exact proportions remain a secret, jealously guarded by each generation of head distiller.

The ingredients that make up Plymouth Gin come from all over the world, a reminder that England's fortunes were built on trade and that Plymouth has always been the ocean gateway for a huge array of exotic produce.

Today only the best botanicals from each crop are selected to give Plymouth Gin its special taste. Micro samples of each batch are rigorously tested until the distiller is satisfied that they are of the highest quality and a perfect match for a consistent flavour.

Only the best botanicals from each crop are selected by the Head Distiller for Plymouth Gin.

ANGELICA ROOT — sweet yet dry

Angelica originated in Iceland, Greenland and northern Russia but the best now comes from Saxony. In Plymouth Gin, angelica root adds musky, woody flavours and contributes to its dryness.

CARDAMOM PODS — aromatic spice

These small pods contain numerous tiny black seeds that have a warm, spicy, aromatic flavour. The cardamom in Plymouth Gin comes from Sri Lanka. After saffron and vanilla, cardamom is the third most expensive spice in the world.

CORIANDER SEEDS — peppery and citrus

Coriander seeds are miniscule fruits and are the second most commonly used botanical in the making of gin. The oil of coriander, released through distillation, has a fresh, slightly spicy, ginger, sage and lemon flavour. Coriander is widely grown in eastern Europe.

JUNIPER BERRIES — distinctive and essential

The main botanical ingredient in all gins, the finest juniper berries are from Italy and from above the tree line in former Yugoslavia. In Plymouth Gin juniper is less obvious than in other gins but its distinctive taste of pine, lavender and camphor is unmistakable.

LEMON PEEL — light, bright and sharp

Citrus peel is used to flavour Plymouth Gin because it, rather than the fruit, contains more valuable oils. Lemon oil is refreshing and invigorating, with many ancient medicinal applications. It contributes a fresh, citrus flavour to Plymouth Gin enhancing its dryness.

ORANGE PEEL — soft rounded citrus flavours

The peel from sweet oranges from southern Spain is used in Plymouth Gin and its dried peel releases an oil that is mildly sedative and often used as an anti-depressant.

ORRIS ROOT — binder of flavours

Orris is the fragrant root of the iris plant commercially grown in Italy. It smells of sweet violets and is used in talcum powder and potpourri mixes. Orris root is ground into a fine powder for use in gin where it imparts earthy, rooty tastes and, like angelica, helps to marry the flavours of the other botanicals.

DRINKING PLYMOUTH GIN

Discover ways to enjoy the flavour of Plymouth Gin.

"Never buy anything less than 40% ABV – you won't get the juniper, sage, citrus flavours of a great gin if you buy a 37.5% ABV brand. Get the greatest, Plymouth." DAVE BROOM, *BBC GOOD FOOD MAGAZINE*, DECEMBER 2001

A Schweppes Tonic label from 1920.

Gin and tonic with a twist.

Gin is becoming increasingly popular with the younger market.

mixed drinks

Commercial production of 'Tonic Brewed Drinks' began as long ago as 1858 when Erasmus Bond patented 'an improved aerated tonic liquid' with quinine and other flavouring agents such as bitter orange. Soon there were many brands of tonic water on the market with Schweppes adding Indian Tonic Water to its range in the 1870s.

Like many other aspects of English culture the gin and tonic dates to the time of the British Raj in India. It came about like this. The principal flavouring of Indian Tonic Water is quinine, from the Peruvian native name for the bark of the cinchona tree, used as cure for fever. In India daily doses of quinine were given to prevent and cure malaria, its unpleasantly bitter flavour masked by sugar, soda water and lemon juice. The addition of gin made it the perfect sundowner and returning colonials brought this exotic combination back home, where it soon caught on.

Although the G&T is still a favourite, there are many other ways of experiencing the taste of Plymouth Gin in delicious, easy to prepare mixed drinks.

raspberry collins
An update on the classic 'Tom Collins'

INGREDIENTS	1 part Plymouth Gin │ 1 part fresh lemon │ 1 part puréed raspberries │ 1/2 part framboise │ 4 parts soda water │ splash of sugar syrup
METHOD	Shake with ice and strain. Top with soda and float framboise. Garnish with lemon slice and raspberries.

"Try a little Plymouth Gin and sparkling mineral water, which in my view makes a far better summer cocktail than London Gin and tonic."

FRANCES BISSELL, *THE TIMES*

Distilled
Dry Gin
is and always has been
absolutely
DRY.
Eminently suitable for
MARTINI
COCKTAILS

The first great age of cocktail drinking.

A Plymouth Gin label for the American market, circa 1950.

Plymouth Gin is a popular cocktail ingredient.

cocktails

The first ever recipe for the classic Dry Martini was published in New York in 1896 in Stuart's *Fancy Drinks & How to Mix Them*. It specified Plymouth Gin, French vermouth and a dash of orange bitters. Plymouth Gin produced its first cocktail book in 1925 and, throughout the 1920s and 1930s, the first great age of cocktail drinking, Plymouth Gin was the gin of choice for the cocktail set, further boosting exports to America, the land of the cocktail. During Prohibition in America private clubs and organisations were allowed to purchase liquor under strict controls and export Plymouth Gin then carried Prohibition stamps to confirm it was legally imported. In the pre-war years gin, particularly Plymouth Gin, became the basis for literally hundreds of white spirit cocktails.

FAMOUS GIN DRINKERS

LORD BYRON "Mad, bad and dangerous to know" Byron was a famous gin drinker who drank his gin mixed with water.

DOROTHY PARKER Famous wit (Dorothy Parker) wrote these lines in honour of the Martini.
"I love to drink martinis
Two at the very most
Three I'm under the table
Four I'm under my host".

mayflower martini

A modern version of the original martini, the Mayflower Martini, is a favourite of Plymouth Gin drinkers.

INGREDIENTS 1/2 part dry vermouth | 3 parts Plymouth Gin
2 dashes of orange bitters or Cointreau

METHOD Stir ingredients in mixing glass with ice. Strain and serve with a twist of lemon.

"Delicate and gauzy…gentle in the land of giants", Hessner said.
DeGroff called it "citrusy and subtle", and Prial found it "soft and fresh".
"This one plays it straight", Asimov said.   *NEW YORK TIMES, APRIL 2003*

pilgrim breeze

INGREDIENTS 2 parts Plymouth Gin
Dash of red vermouth | Orange juice
Cranberry juice

METHOD Build ingredients into a tall
glass topping with equal measures
of orange & cranberry juices.
Garnish with a wedge of lime.

devon lemonade

INGREDIENTS 2 parts Plymouth Gin
1 part Elderflower cordial | Sparkling
water | Mint and lemon to garnish

METHOD Pour the gin and elder-
flower into a tall glass, add the mint
and plenty of ice, and top up with
sparkling water. Garnish with a slice
of lemon.

gimlet

INGREDIENTS 3 parts Plymouth Gin
1 part Rose's lime juice | Lime
wedge to garnish

METHOD Stir with ice and strain into
a chilled cocktail glass. Garnish with
a lime wedge.

red snapper

Invented by Harry MacElhone at
Harry's New York Bar. He is also
famous for the invention of the
the Bloody Mary.

INGREDIENTS   1 pinch salt, white pepper, celery salt (optional) | dash of
Tabasco & Worcester sauce | 1/2 part lemon juice | 2 parts
Plymouth Gin | 4 parts tomato juice | dash of ruby port

METHOD   Build in hiball glass over ice and stir. Garnish with celery
stick and lemon slice.

> "I like to use Plymouth Gin...its flavour is better - more delicately aromatic – than other gin's."
>
> NIGELLA LAWSON, *FOREVER SUMMER*, 2002

subliminal scallops

INGREDIENTS 450g shelled scallops
4 tbsp. butter | 1 tbsp. olive oil
125g flour | 185g Plymouth Gin
Juice of a lime | 1 large knob of
ginger finely sliced | 2 tsps Thai fish
sauce | 240ml cream | Large pinch
saffron | 3 cloves of chopped garlic
Small bunch chopped coriander

A TASTE OF
THE WEST COUNTRY

Plymouth Gin combines very well with many different types of food, particularly those spicy, smoky and sweet flavours where the dryness of the gin enhances the intensity of the taste. We've given some suggested recipes on this page and the next.

At the distillery there is also the opportunity to sample a range of local West Country produce from smoked fish and meats to unusual chutneys and preserves.

METHOD Combine cream and saffron and reserve. Combine gin, lime juice, fish sauce and sliced ginger and reserve. Lightly flour scallops. Brown garlic in butter and olive oil in large frying pan or wok. Add scallops and cook for about 3 minutes. Add gin mixture and cook to thicken slightly. Add cream mixture and continue cooking for 2-4 minutes. Serve immediately on a bed of rice and sprinkle coriander on top.

"My absolute favourite is Plymouth Gin which is beautifully balanced, with soft, moreish, almost sweet flavours and scents of citrus fruit and flowers." SUSY ATKINS, *THE EXPRESS*, 13 MAY 2000

rhubarb sorbet with plymouth classic fruit cup

INGREDIENTS 400g rhubarb
4 dessertspoons caster sugar.
(Be sure to use white sugar to retain the pink in the rhubarb). | 250ml orange jelly | 10g unsalted butter
250ml Plymouth Classic Fruit Cup

© JULIE DONVIN-IRONS

METHOD Clean and chop the rhubarb into chunks. Melt the butter in a pan on a medium heat. Add the rhubarb, stirring regularly until it is completely soft. Add the sugar, turn the heat down low, and place a lid on the pan and cook for a further 5 minutes until the sugar has dissolved. Remove from the pan and allow to cool. Meanwhile, dissolve the orange jelly in 250ml of hot water. When completely dissolved, mix well with the rhubarb. Add the Plymouth Classic Fruit Cup and stir in well. Cool, then pour into individual serving dishes and place in the freezer for about 4 hours.

strawberry and plymouth classic fruit cup crumble

INGREDIENTS 400g strawberries
125g caster sugar | 150ml Plymouth Classic Fruit Cup
Crumble mixture: 75g unsalted butter | 75g demerara sugar
150g plain flour

© JULIE DONVIN-IRONS

METHOD Pre heat the oven to 400°F/gas 6/200°C. Cut the straw-berries into chunks and place in a large bowl, sprinkle with caster sugar and pour over the Plymouth Classic Fruit Cup. In another bowl, place the flour and sugar, then dice the butter into it. Rub butter, flour and sugar together to make crumbs. Put the strawberry mixture into 4 ramekin dishes then evenly distribute the crumble mix over each one. Bake in hot oven for about 20 minutes, until the topping is golden brown. Serve warm or cold with Devonshire double cream for a real taste of Plymouth in Devon.

pineapple & plymouth damson liqueur upside down cake

INGREDIENTS 3 tbsp. Plymouth Damson Liqueur | 2 tbsp. golden syrup | 1 small can pineapple rings
115g butter or margarine
115g caster sugar | 2 eggs
170g self raising flour | little milk to mix if necessary

© JULIE DONVIN-IRONS

METHOD Pre heat oven to 350°F/gas 4/180°C. Line an 18cm greased cake tin with greaseproof paper. Fill base of tin with golden syrup, pineapple rings, and 2 tbsp. Damson Liqueur. In a large bowl cream the butter and sugar then beat in eggs. Fold in flour and add milk if it is too thick. Put mixture into tin and bake 25-30 mins. Remove from oven and turn out upside down onto a warmed plate. Sprinkle the remaining Damson Liqueur over the pineapple. Serve warm with Devonshire double cream and a glass of Plymouth Damson Liqueur or Sloe Gin.

Sloe Motion
3/4 shot Plymouth Sloe Gin in a champagne flute and top up with chilled champagne.

Dam–Shame
3/4 shot Plymouth Damson Liqueur in a champagne flute and top with chilled champagne.

Plymouth Classic Fruit Cup

FRUIT GINS, LIQUEURS AND CUPS

"My favourite choice for afternoons in the garden is the Classic Fruit Cup from Plymouth Gin."

ANDREW CATCHPOLE,
THE DAILY TELEGRAPH

A recipe book, dated 1832, at the Black Friars Distillery confirms that Coates & Co., like many other distillers at the time, made a variety of fruit gins, cordials and liqueurs such as Peppermint Gin, Lemon Gin and Lovage, a popular cordial made with oils of nutmeg, caraway and cassia.

Plymouth Sloe Gin has long been produced at Black Friars. For many years the company also produced the gin base for Hawkers Sloe Gin - possibly the connection starting with the partner of Coates & Co., William Henry Hawker, who was also involved in the Hawker wine and spirit business.

Sloe Gin is a traditional British liqueur, much loved by the hunting, shooting and fishing set. It is made by steeping wild sloe berries, the fruit of the blackthorn tree, in domestic strength Plymouth Gin. The alcoholic strength is then reduced to around 26% abv. Damson Liqueur is made in a similar process using damson plums instead of sloe berries. Both are delicious either as an accompaniment to cheese instead of Port, as an after dinner drink, or in cocktails and mixed drinks.

Fruit Cups were widely drunk in the 19th century and were traditionally gin based. Today Pimms is the most well known Fruit Cup although in recent years its strength has been cut. Plymouth Classic Fruit Cup has full strength Plymouth Gin at its heart, blended with a unique selection of fruits, liqueurs and bitters.
A traditional summer drink, it is best served in a large jug topped up with lemonade, or ginger ale for a less sweet flavour.